To:_____

From:_____

Date:_____

The Jesus With Us Series is dedicated to showing children how much He loves them and that He is always with them. This awareness will develop faith and confidence, paving the way for a brighter future.
— S&L

Copyright © 2022 by Sybrand & Lucia. All rights reserved.
Published by Ciana Publishers.

This Book is Copyright Protected:

This is only for personal use. You cannot amend, distribute, sell, use, quote, or paraphrase any part of the content within this book without the consent of the authors. The Authors guarantee all contents are original and do not infringe upon the legal rights of any other person or work.

No part of this book may be reproduced, duplicated, or transmitted in any form by means such as printing, scanning, photocopying, or otherwise, without direct written permission from the authors or publisher, except for the use of quotations in a book review and as permitted by the U.S. copyright law. For permission, contact info@cianapublishers.com.

Disclaimer and Terms of Use:
This book is provided solely for spiritual upliftment, entertainment, motivational and informational purposes.

All Scripture quotations, unless otherwise indicated, are taken from the Holy Bible, New International Version®, NIV®. Copyright ©1973, 1978, 1984, 2011 by Biblica, Inc.™ Used by permission of Zondervan. All rights reserved worldwide. www.zondervan.com The "NIV" and "New International Version" are trademarks registered in the United States Patent and Trademark Office by Biblica, Inc.™

Authors - Sybrand JvR & Lucia S

cianapublishers.com

THE RHYME OF THE PRODIGAL SON IS BASED ON LUKE 15:11-32

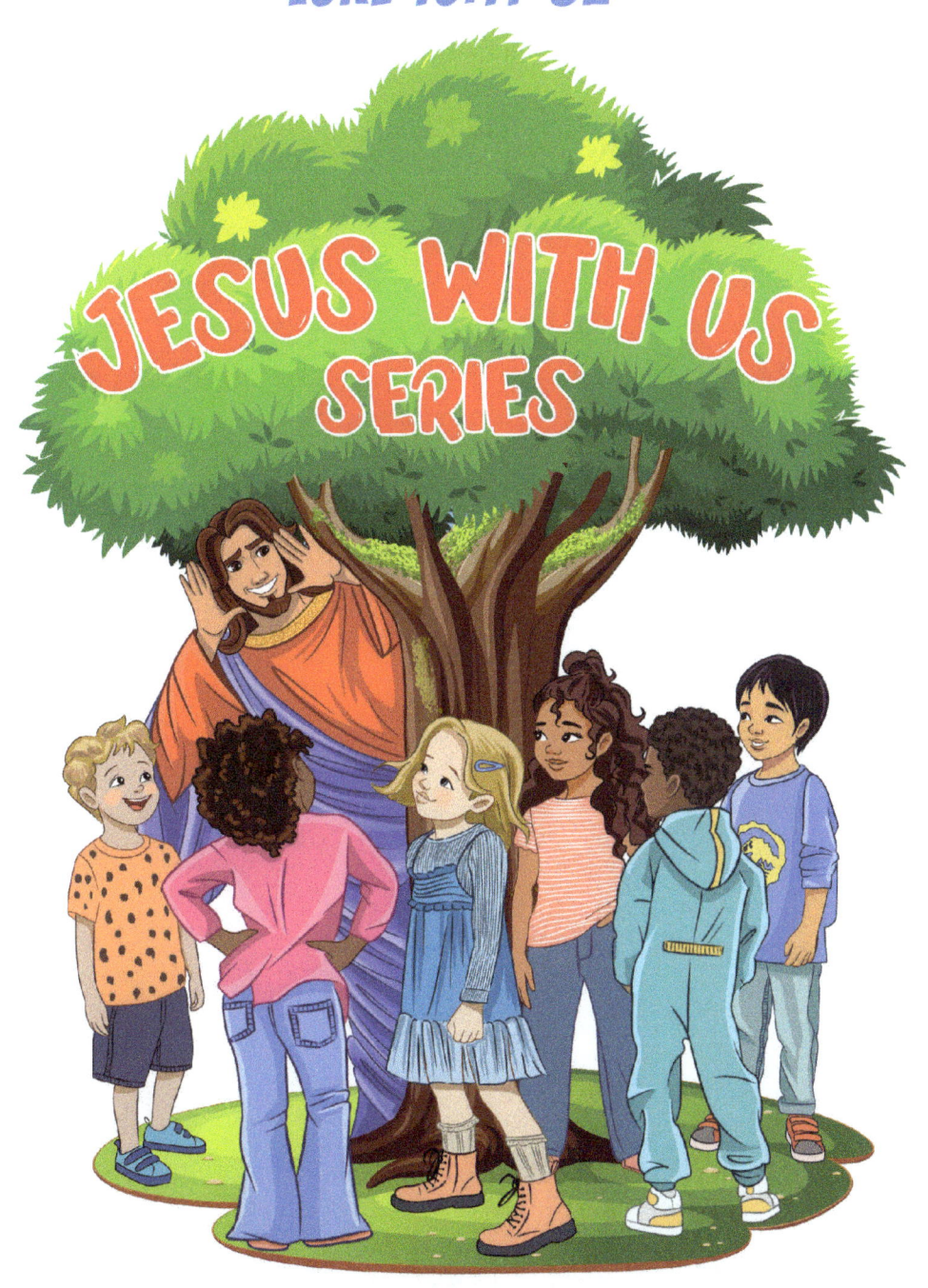

A father had two boys from the Lord.
Both handsome and healthy, but one so bored.
He thought this world just had to be explored.

He begged and pleaded, "I'm grown."
"This is my time to make it on my own."
"I can't wait to explore the unknown."

"Father! Give me what I desire."
"I want my piece of this empire."
"I'm ready to live life higher."

Dad gave in and said, "Take care, my son."
"I'll wish you well, though this isn't fun."
His son replied, "My life has just begun."

He spent what he had on friend and foe.
He paraded his riches and let them flow.
After years of fun, he had nothing to show.

His money ran out, and his friends said, "Cheers!"
"It's been great knowing you all these years."
He was left heartbroken and in tears.

He returned to his father, full of blame.
Thinking of his guilt and his shame.
He could only see who he became.

The older son said, "I've not received a celebration."
"How could my father forgive my brother's violation?"
"I have been good and not given into temptation."

The older brother refused to go in.
His father went out and pleaded with him.
"Be grateful and thankful and look within."

"Everything I have belongs to you."
"Just think of all we've been through."
"Can you not see how much I love you?"

"Your brother was lost, but now he's found."
"My joy is full and knows no bound."
"Join us to make a joyful sound."

Praise the Lord!
We all make mistakes.
There is nobody who doesn't make mistakes.
The question is, what do you do after you have made a mistake?

Jesus is like the father, who does not keep a record of your mistakes. He accepts you as if you have never done anything wrong. When you go to Jesus over your wrong, He stands with open arms to welcome you.

Although The Prodigal Son left his father's house, his room was never given away. His father kept his room, hopeful that he would return home. Jesus always keeps your room safe within. Know that Jesus loves you and welcomes you. In Jesus' house, you will always have your own room.

When you make a mistake, as we all do, don't run from Jesus but quickly return to Him. Like the father, Jesus runs with open arms to meet you. Your room has your name on it.
No one but you can occupy it.

Tell somebody. "Return Home!"

Dear Jesus.

Thank you for Your precious love.
And all You give me from above.

Thank you for forgiving me each time I sin.
And for keeping my room safe within.

In Jesus' name.

Amen! Amen! Amen!

LUKE 15:20-24 NIV

20 So he got up and went to his father.
"But while he was still a long way off,
his father saw him and was filled
with compassion for him;
he ran to his son,
threw his arms around him
and kissed him.

21 "The son said to him,
'Father, I have sinned
against heaven and against you.
I am no longer worthy to be
called your son.'

22 "But the father said to his servants,
'Quick! Bring the best robe and put it on him.
Put a ring on his finger and sandals on his feet.

23 Bring the fattened calf and kill it.
Let's have a feast and celebrate.

24 For this son of mine was
dead and is alive again;
he was lost and is found.'
So they began to celebrate.

FOR FURTHER READING: LUKE 15:11-32

LET'S CHAT

Do you think it is good for you to receive everything you ask for, as The Prodigal Son did? ____
_____
_____

How can friends influence your life? How do you influence your friends? _____
_____
_____

Do your friends gain from you as much as you gain from them? We are referring to your kindness, friendliness, etc. _____
_____
_____

Are you thankful for what you have, or are you only complaining about what you don't have?
_____
_____

What can you say about how the older brother reacted? _____
_____
_____

After reading this book, how do you feel about going to Jesus after making a mistake?
_____
_____

What can you say about the fact that in Jesus' house, no one else can stay in your room? ____
_____
_____

WORDS IN THE RHYME MADE EASY TO UNDERSTAND

Parables:
Stories told by Jesus to teach us how to be good and to tell us more about His Kingdom, His Father, and Heaven.

Prodigal:
In the rhyme, 'prodigal' means, 'It's somebody who's been gone for a long period, did some bad stuff, and then returned home.'

Explored:
In the rhyme, 'explored' means, 'To go and visit other countries.'

Empire:
In the rhyme, 'empire' means, 'All the land, money, and stuff that belongs to the father.'

Live life higher:
In the rhyme, 'live life higher' means, 'The Prodigal Son wants to live a lavish lifestyle of free-spending.'

Foe:
In the rhyme, 'foe' means, 'Someone who is not a friend.

Paraded:
In the rhyme, 'paraded' means, 'The Prodigal Son shows off how much money he has and spends it foolishly.'

Heartbroken:
In the rhyme, 'heartbroken' means, 'The Prodigal Son was very sad, having no friends or money.'

Greed:
In the rhyme, 'greed' means, 'The Prodigal Son was only thinking of himself in wanting something so badly that he didn't consider the feelings of others.'

Shame:
In the rhyme, 'shame' means, 'The Prodigal Son felt so bad because of the wrong he did.'

Violation:
Doing what is wrong. Breaking the rules.

Temptation:
In the rhyme, 'temptation' means, 'This is something that is not good for you, and you should stay away from it, but it keeps inviting you.' Also, read (Genesis 4:7).

Knows no bound:
In the rhyme, 'knows no bound' means, 'Nothing is holding back the father's joy. He is very happy.'

OTHER BOOKS IN THE JESUS WITH US SERIES

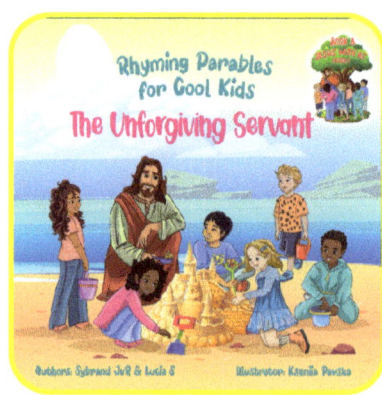
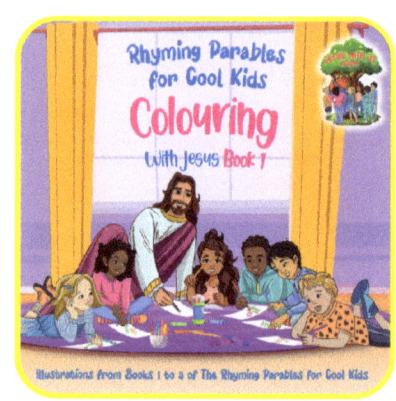

SCAN ME

OTHER BOOKS BY THE AUTHORS

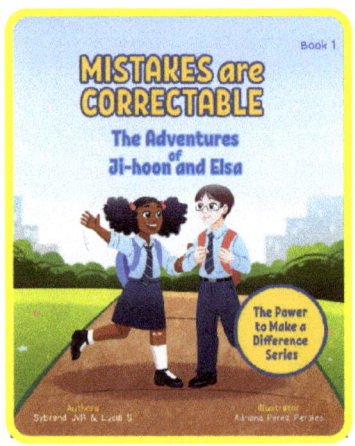
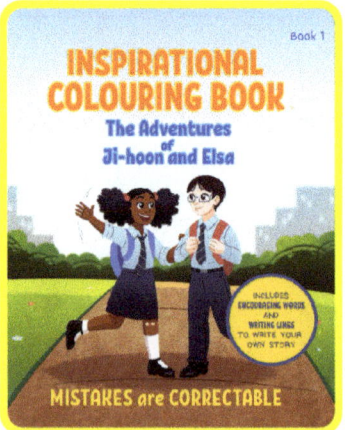

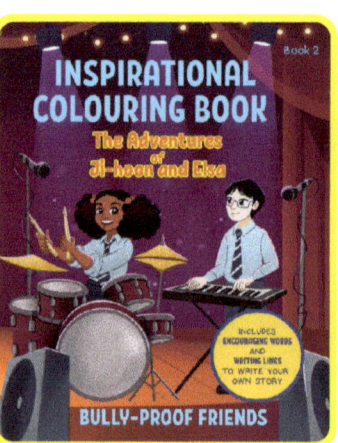